C000282578

by Iain Gray

Lang Syne

PUBLISHING

WRITING *to* REMEMBER

Lang**Syne**

PUBLISHING

WRITING *to* REMEMBER

79 Main Street, Newtongrange,
Midlothian EH22 4NA
Tel: 0131 344 0414   Fax: 0845 075 6085
E-mail: info@lang-syne.co.uk
www.langsyneshop.co.uk

Design by Dorothy Meikle
Printed by Printwell Ltd
© Lang Syne Publishers Ltd 2016

ISBN 978-1-85217-217-6

Paterson

MOTTO:
Huc Tendimus Omnes
(We all strive for this)

CREST:
A dexter hand issuing
out of a cloud holding
a branch of laurel, all Proper

Echoes of a far distant past
can still be found in most names

Chapter one:

Origins of Scottish surnames

by George Forbes

It all began with the Normans.

For it was they who introduced surnames into common usage more than a thousand years ago, initially based on the title of their estates, local villages and chateaux in France to distinguish and identify these landholdings, usually acquired at the point of a bloodstained sword.

Such grand descriptions also helped enhance the prestige of these arrogant warlords and generally glorify their lofty positions high above the humble serfs slaving away below in the pecking order who only had single names, often with Biblical connotations as in Pierre and Jacques.

The only descriptive distinctions among this peasantry concerned their occupations, like Pierre the swineherd or Jacques the ferryman.

The Normans themselves were originally Vikings (or Northmen) who raided, colonised and eventually settled down around the French coastline.

They had sailed up the Seine in their longboats in 900AD under their ferocious leader Rollo and ruled the roost in north east France before sailing over to conquer England, bringing their relatively new tradition of having surnames with them.

It took another hundred years for the Normans to percolate northwards and surnames did not begin to appear in Scotland until the thirteenth century.

These adventurous knights brought an aura of chivalry with them and it was said no damsel of any distinction would marry a man unless he had at least two names.

The family names included that of Scotland's great hero Robert De Brus and his compatriots were warriors from families like the De Morevils, De Umphravils, De Berkelais, De Quincis, De Viponts and De Vaux.

As the knights settled the boundaries of

their vast estates, they took territorial names, as in Hamilton, Moray, Crawford, Cunningham, Dunbar, Ross, Wemyss, Dundas, Galloway, Renfrew, Greenhill, Hazelwood, Sandylands and Church-hill.

Other names, though not with any obvious geographical or topographical features, nevertheless derived from ancient parishes like Douglas, Forbes, Dalyell and Guthrie.

Other surnames were coined in connection with occupations, castles or legendary deeds. Stuart originated in the word steward, a prestigious post which was an integral part of any large medieval household. The same applied to Cooks, Chamberlains, Constables and Porters.

Borders towns and forts – needed in areas like the Debateable Lands which were constantly fought over by feuding local families – had their own distinctive names; and it was often from them that the resident groups took their communal titles, as in the Grahams of Annandale, the Elliots and Armstrongs of the East Marches, the Scotts and Kerrs of Teviotdale and Eskdale.

Even physical attributes crept into surnames, as in Small, Little and More (the latter being 'beg' in Gaelic), Long or Lang, Stark, Stout, Strong or Strang and even Jolly.

Mieklejohns would have had the strength of several men, while Littlejohn was named after the legendary sidekick of Robin Hood.

Colours got into the act with Black, White, Grey, Brown and Green (Red developed into Reid, Ruddy or Ruddiman). Blue was rare and nobody ever wanted to be associated with yellow.

Pompous worthies took the name Wiseman, Goodman and Goodall.

Words intimating the sons of leading figures were soon affiliated into the language as in Johnson, Adamson, Richardson and Thomson, while the Norman equivalent of Fitz (from the French-Latin 'filius' meaning 'son') cropped up in Fitzmaurice and Fitzgerald.

The prefix 'Mac' was 'son of' in Gaelic and clans often originated with occupations – as in MacNab being sons of the Abbot, MacPherson and MacVicar being sons of the minister and MacIntosh being sons of the chief.

The church's influence could be found in the names Kirk, Clerk, Clarke, Bishop, Friar and Monk. Proctor came from a church official, Singer and Sangster from choristers, Gilchrist and Gillies from Christ's servant, Mitchell, Gilmory and Gilmour from servants of St Michael and Mary, Malcolm from a servant of Columba and Gillespie from a bishop's servant.

The rudimentary medical profession was represented by Barber (a trade which also once included dentistry and surgery) as well as Leech or Leitch.

Businessmen produced Merchants, Mercers, Monypennies, Chapmans, Sellers and Scales, while down at the old village watermill the names that cropped up included Miller, Walker and Fuller.

Other self explanatory trades included Coopers, Brands, Barkers, Tanners, Skinners, Brewsters and Brewers, Tailors, Saddlers, Wrights, Cartwrights, Smiths, Harpers, Joiners, Sawyers, Masons and Plumbers.

Even the scenery was utilised as in Craig, Moor, Hill, Glen, Wood and Forrest.

Rank, whether high or low, took its place with Laird, Barron, Knight, Tennant, Farmer, Husband, Granger, Grieve, Shepherd, Shearer and Fletcher.

The hunt and the chase supplied Hunter, Falconer, Fowler, Fox, Forrester, Archer and Spearman.

The renowned medieval historian Froissart, who eulogised about the romantic deeds of chivalry (and who condemned Scotland as being a poverty stricken wasteland), once sniffily dismissed the peasantry of his native France as the jacquerie (or the jacques-without-names) but it was these same humble folk who ended up over-throwing the arrogant aristocracy.

In the olden days, only the blueblooded knights of antiquity were entitled to full, proper names, both Christian and surnames, but with the passing of time and a more egalitarian, less feudal atmosphere, more respectful and worthy titles spread throughout the populace as a whole.

Echoes of a far distant past can still be found in most names and they can be borne with pride in commemoration of past generations who fought and toiled in some capacity or other to make our nation what it now is, for good or ill.

Chapter two:

The sons of Patrick

The origin of the surname Paterson, in all its rich variety of spellings, stretches back through the mists of time to no less a figure than St. Patrick, the patron saint of Ireland.

The origins of the famous saint himself remain shrouded in historical obscurity, but it is believed he was born about 389A.D. in either Britain or Gaul.

Also believed to have been of royal birth, this explains why 'Patrick' means 'scion of a noble family.'

Kidnapped by pirates at an early age, he lived for a time on the continent before embarking on his apostolic mission to Ireland, where he died around 461A.D.

One of the Church's earliest saints, St. Patrick gained devotees not only in Ireland, but also throughout Christianised Europe, and Patrick became a popular forename.

In Scotland, and for curious reasons that have now been lost, Patrick was also considered to be a form of Peter, another popular forename that derived from St. Peter, and for many centuries the names were synonymous.

In common with many names, the forename, or Christian name, of Patrick gradually evolved into a surname, taking forms that include Paterson ('son of Patrick'), Patterson, Patrickson, Patersoun, Patrison, Peterson, and Patison.

Paterson (with a single 't') is the most common form of the name found in Scotland, with Patterson (with two 't's) predominating in the north of England.

The name also boasts a number of Gaelic variations that were found throughout the length and breadth of the Highlands and Islands.

The most common of these forms was MacPatrick ('son of Patrick'), while others included MacPhedran, MacFetridge, MacFater, MacPhater, and MacFeat.

Another Gaelic rendering of Paterson was 'Pheadirean', and a Clan Pheadirean, believed to

have had ancestral homelands on the north side of
Loch Fyne, is believed to have been a sept, or
branch, of Clan MacAulay.

The relationship with the MacAulays
remains obscure, but much stronger links can be
identified between the MacPatricks/Patersons
and the proud Highland clans of MacLaren
and Lamont.

Any Patersons of today who can trace a
descent from the homelands of these two clans
may well be entitled to share in their rich heritage
and traditions.

It is with Clan MacLaren, whose homelands were around Balquhidder and Strathearn,
in Perthshire, that the Paterson bond is particularly strong.

A lion bearing a crown and wreathed with
laurel is the crest, and 'The boar's rock', is the
motto of this clan that claims a descent from Lorn,
a son of the royal Irish warrior Fergus Erc, who
settled in the area of present day Argyll, on the
west coast of Scotland, in the early years of the
sixth century.

Also known as the Clan Labhruinn, it is believed the name MacLaren may also be traced back to the Celtic abbot Labhran of Ardveche.

One curious legend relates that the MacPatrick/Paterson link with the clan arose when numerous clans had vied for the skills of a renowned smith by the name of MacPatrick.

The art of smithing, more popularly known today as blacksmithing, was vital to the community of clans not only for forging agricultural and household implements, but also for deadly weapons of war.

The legend relates that the MacLarens were successful in obtaining the valued skills of MacPatrick and that his descendants subsequently became a branch, or sept, of the clan.

There may well be a basis of truth to this legend, although it should be pointed out that the vast majority of smiths who carried out their art in the Highlands and Islands bore the surname of Gow, the Gaelic rendering of Smith.

By whatever means the link between the MacPatricks/MacLarens came about, however, it

is known with certainty that throughout the long
centuries of Scotland's turbulent history they
shared in both the clan's glorious fortunes and
tragic misfortunes.

As kinsfolk of the MacLaren clansfolk
they were destined to be at the forefront of
not only the nation's bitter and bloody wars of
independence against England, but also stalwart
adherents of the Royal House of Stuart.

A contingent of MacLarens and their
kinsmen such as the Patersons are known to have
fought with distinction at the battle of
Bannockburn in June of 1314, when a 20,000-
strong English army under Edward II was defeated
by a Scots army less than half this strength.

By midsummer of 1313 the mighty
fortress of Stirling Castle was occupied by an
English garrison under the command of Sir Philip
Mowbray and Bruce's brother, Edward, agreed to
a pledge by the commander that if the castle was
not relieved by battle by midsummer of the following year, then he would surrender.

This made battle inevitable, and by June

23 of 1314 the two armies faced one another at Bannockburn, in sight of the castle.

It was on this day that Bruce slew the English knight Sir Henry de Bohun in single combat, but the battle proper was not fought until the following day, shortly after the rise of the midsummer sun.

The English cavalry launched a desperate but futile charge on the densely packed ranks of Scottish spearmen known as schiltrons, and by the time the sun had sank slowly in the west the English army had been totally routed.

In September of 1513, MacLarens and their kinsfolk such as the Patersons were among the 5,000 Scots including James IV, an archbishop, two bishops, eleven earls, fifteen barons, and 300 knights who were killed at the disastrous battle of Flodden.

The Scottish monarch had embarked on the venture after Queen Anne of France, under the terms of the Auld Alliance between Scotland and her nation, appealed to him to 'break a lance' on her behalf and act as her chosen knight.

Crossing the border into England at the head of a 25,000-strong army that included 7,500 clansmen and their kinsmen, James engaged a 20,000-strong force commanded by the Earl of Surrey.

Despite their numerical superiority and bravery, however, the Scots proved no match for the skilled English artillery and superior military tactics of Surrey.

Nearly thirty-five years later, in 1547, MacLarens and their kinsmen such as the Patersons also fought and died for their nation at the equally disastrous battle of Pinkie, near Musselburgh, on Scotland's east coast, following the invasion of a 25,000-strong English army under the Duke of Somerset.

The MacLarens were among the 3,000 clansmen and their kinsmen who fought under the leadership of the Earl of Argyll and who were either killed on the battlefield or were forced to flee to safety.

In later centuries, the Patersons would again find themselves embroiled in mighty power struggles as a series of divisive and destructive civil wars swept the nation.

Chapter three:

Crown and Covenant

A kinship can also be claimed between the MacPatricks/Patersons and Clan Lamont, and the reasons for this are rooted in tragedy.

Bearers of an ancient Celtic pedigree that can be traced back to a branch of the royal house of the O'Neils of Ulster, the Lamonts, whose motto is 'Neither spare nor disgrace', and whose crest is an upright right hand, palm facing outwards, were in possession of the bulk of the territory of Cowal, in Argyll, well before the twelfth century.

Among their neighbours were the powerful Campbells of Argyll, and the two clans engaged in a series of bloody clashes as the Campbells encroached on Lamont territory, while they took opposing sides in the bitter civil war that raged between Crown and Covenant in the mid seventeenth century.

The Covenanters took their name from

the National Covenant, signed in 1638, and which pledged to uphold the Presbyterian religion.

Opposed to the divine right of kings as expressed by Charles I, the Covenanters were soon at war with the Royalist forces of the monarch.

Archibald Campbell, 8th Earl of Argyll, chief of the Campbells, and later Marquis of Argyll, was one of the main leaders of the Covenanting party, and it was in recognition of this that in March of 1643 Charles I issued a special commission to his loyal supporter Sir James Lamont of Inveryne, the Lamont chief.

His royal remit was 'to prosecute a war and levy forces in His Majesty's name against those in rebellion, and particularly against the Marquis of Argyll.'

It was an opportunity for the Lamont chief to not only serve his king, but to strike a blow against his hated neighbour. He set about his task with zeal, ravaging the Campbell lands.

The Campbells were destined to exact a horrific revenge for these atrocities only a few short years later.

Royalist hopes effectively died with the defeat of the forces of the Marquis of Montrose at the battle of Philiphaugh in September of 1645, and the subsequent surrender of the king himself to a Scots army in May of the following year.

Sir James Lamont disbanded the forces he had raised and returned to his stronghold of Toward Castle, south of Inellan, while a triumphant Marquis of Argyll made himself the master of Scotland.

His forces laid siege to Toward, forcing Sir James to surrender it on June 3, 1646.

His reluctant surrender came only after he had received a solemn assurance that his kinsfolk would not be molested and the Lamont estates spared from plunder and destruction.

No sooner had the surrender terms been agreed than Sir James and some of his closest relatives were imprisoned, while about 200 of his kinsfolk were rounded up, thrown into boats, and taken north to Dunoon.

Arriving at a hill outside the town, thirty-eight men described as 'leading gentlemen' of the

Lamonts, were hanged from an ash tree that grew behind a nearby churchyard.

Taken down while still alive, they were cast into hastily dug pits, while the rest of the prisoners, including women and children and the elderly, were stabbed and bludgeoned and also thrown into the pits.

The frenzied orgies of bloodlust over, the pits were covered with earth, leaving those still alive to slowly suffocate to death.

Surviving Lamonts were either driven from their ancestral lands or forced to assume new identities by taking on new surnames, such as Paterson, and any Patersons of today who can trace a descent back to Cowal, in Argyll, could well be descendants of these original Lamonts.

While many MacPatricks, through their kinship with the Lamonts, took the part of the House of Stuart in the wars between Crown and Covenant, many of their Lowland counterparts were firmly identified with the cause of the Covenanters.

With many Covenanters literally forced

to take to the hills to practise their Presbyterian religion, hundreds were hunted down by government troops.

Robert Paterson was killed at the battle of Aird's Moss, in Ayrshire, in 1680, along with the charismatic Covenanting leader Richard Cameron, while his son, William, was captured in 1684 and forcibly enlisted into the armed forces and sent abroad.

He managed to escape, however, and returned to Scotland to renew his fight on behalf of the Covenant, only to be recaptured and executed.

Alexander Paterson, from Muirkirk, in Ayrshire, was among 201 Covenanter prisoners who drowned while being transported to Barbados to be sold as slaves after being captured at the battle of Bothwell Brig.

A total of 250 prisoners had been packed aboard the *Crown of London*, which sailed for the colonies from Leith in November of 1679.

Anchoring off Orkney on December 10, the ship dragged its anchor during a severe storm

Raising the Standard at Glenfinnan

and foundered on rocks overlooked by cliffs at the Mull of Deerness.

The crew made their escape from the stricken vessel, but not before locking the hatches that held Paterson and his fellow prisoners.

Some managed to escape, but many fell to their deaths as they were forced back by their captors as they attempted to scale the cliffs.

Ironically, the Leith merchant who had owned the vessel that had carried Paterson and his fellow prisoners to their deaths was a William Paterson.

Robert Paterson, born at Hawick, in the Borders, in 1715, has gained immortality as Sir Walter Scott's famous character 'Old Mortality', for the painstaking work he carried out in erecting and maintaining the hundreds of memorials to Covenanter martyrs.

A skilled stonemason, Paterson, who died in Dumfriesshire in 1801, dedicated about fifty years of his life to caring for these monuments that can still be seen scattered throughout the landscape of southwest Scotland

The wars between Crown and Covenant finally drew to an exhausted close around 1688, but further bitter and bloody conflict was still in store for both the Lowland Patersons and their Highland counterparts through their allegiance to the cause of the Royal House of Stuart.

The Standard of the exiled Royal House was raised when Prince Charles Edward Stuart, known as the Young Pretender, arrived on Scottish shores in July of 1745.

Rallying loyal support, a great victory followed at the battle of Prestonpans in September, and a confident Jacobite army left Edinburgh for the march on London at the end of October, only to controversially retire back north in early December after reaching Derby.

Foremost among those Patersons loyal to the Stuart cause was Sir Hugh Paterson of Bannockburn, who entertained the prince in his mansion of Bannockburn House, near Stirling, in January of 1746.

It was here that the prince met Sir Hugh's young niece, Clementina Walkinshaw, igniting a passion so strong that she followed him in 1751 to his lonely exile in France.

The couple never married but Clementina bore him a daughter, Charlotte, whom the prince in later years created Duchess of Albany.

As *The Bonnie Lass O' Albany*, she became the subject of a moving poem by Scotland's national bard Robert Burns.

At the disastrous battle of Culloden, fought on Drummossie Moor, near Inverness, on April 16th, 1746, MacLarens and their kinsmen such as the Macpatricks/Patersons, fought with distinction for the doomed Jacobite cause under the colours of the Stewarts of Appin Regiment.

Chapter four:

On the world stage

Far from the field of battle, generations of Patersons have flourished in a number of rather more peaceful pursuits.

Born at Tynwald, Dumfriesshire, in 1658, William Paterson was the farmer's son who, after a successful career as a merchant, founded the world-renowned Bank of England in 1694 after settling in London.

While the banking venture continues to thrive to this day, another scheme launched by Paterson proved decidedly less successful: this was the infamous Darien Scheme, a bold attempt to set up a Scottish trading company near present-day Panama.

A combination of factors wrecked all chance of the scheme succeeding, however, and it was finally abandoned in 1699, just over a year after the first vessels had sailed from Scotland on the venture.

A heartbroken Paterson also lost his wife

and child, who had accompanied him on the expedition to the malarial infested swamps on Panama.

He died in 1719, and despite the failure of the Darien scheme he is recognised today as one of the earliest advocates of free trade, along with fellow Scotsman Adam Smith.

In the world of politics, William Paterson, born in 1745 in County Antrim and who immigrated to America with his family at the tender age of two, became a New Jersey statesman and one of the signatories of the American Constitution.

A graduate of Princeton University, he also gave his name to Paterson, in New Jersey, and William Paterson University.

Andrew Barton Paterson, better known as 'Banjo' Paterson, was the eldest son of a family from Lanarkshire, in Scotland, who found a new life in Australia. Born at Narambla, near Orange, New South Wales, in 1864, he became a practising lawyer, but is better known as the poet responsible for penning the famous *Waltzing Matilda*.

In the world of sport, Floyd Patterson is the American champion boxer who was born in

Brooklyn in 1935. Aged only 17, he won a gold medal at the 1952 Helsinki Olympics as a middleweight, while in 1956 he became the youngest world heavyweight champion in boxing history when he defeated Archie Moor for the title.

Patterson, who retired from boxing in 1972, is a member of the prestigious International Boxing Hall of Fame and is the proud possessor of a record of 55 wins, 40 wins by knockout, one draw, and only eight losses.

In the world of books, James B. Patterson, born in 1947, is the best-selling American author whose main fictional creation is the forensic psychologist Alex Cross.

A number of his books have been made into successful films starring American actor Morgan Freeman, including *Kiss the Girls* and *Along Came a Spider*.

Still in contemporary times, Tim Paterson, born in 1956, is the American computer programmer credited with the popular MS-DOS operating system.